COLUMBIA COLLEGE CHICAGO

3 2711 00117 7405

Columbia College Library
600 South Michigan
Chicago, IL 60605

W9-CLN-970

Landscape with Silos

Deborah Bogen

Texas Review Press
Huntsville, Texas

ENTERED MAR 1 2 2007

Copyright © 2006 by Deborah Bogen
All rights reserved
Printed in the United States of America

FIRST EDITION, 2006

Requests for permission to reproduce material from this work should
be sent to:

> Permissions
> Texas Review Press
> English Department
> Sam Houston State University
> Huntsville, TX 77341-2146

Acknowledgments:

Grateful acknowledgment is made to the following journals in which
some of these poems (some with different titles or in slightly different
forms) first appeared: *Art-Life, Black Buzzard Review, Buckle&, Crate,
Field, Iron Horse Literary Review, JAMA (Journal of the American Medical
Association), Lyric, MARGIE, Peregrine, Pittsburgh Post Gazette, Poetry
International, Rivendell, Shenandoah, The Indiana Review,* and *The Santa
Monica Review.*

In addition, some of these poems appeared in the chapbook *Living by
the Children's Cemetery,* ByLine Press, 2002.

Heartfelt thanks to Betty Adcock, Doug Anderson, Jim Bogen,
Chris Buckley, Anthony Butts, Lynn Emanuel, David Firman, Stuart
Friebert, Carol Frost, Robert Nazarene, Paul Ruffin, David Young,
Jean Valentine, Michael Woodcock, and the Monday Night Writing
Group—midwives all.

Cover design by Paul Ruffin

Library of Congress Cataloging-in-Publication Data

Bogen, Deborah, 1950-
  Landscape with silos / Deborah Bogen.-- 1st ed.
    p. cm.
  ISBN-13: 978-1-881515-93-7 (pbk. : alk. paper)
  ISBN-10: 1-881515-93-1 (pbk. : alk. paper) 1. Free verse. I. Title.
  PS3602.O425L36 2006
  811'.6--dc22
                        2006000841

for Jim,

who changed my mind

Table of Contents

Learning the Language

The Poem Ventures Out

Visitations

Within the Porcelain Theater

Learning the Language

Dakota is everywhere.
A condition.
And I am only a device of memory.

[Thomas McGrath]

Moving the Moon

I'm not interested in the shaggy horse
(or is it a pony?) although it's white.
It's usually dirty, comes into my mind with steam
rising from thick fur.

I close the gate, improvise some
dark green and black, an undifferentiated
thickness above which I put a moon
for accent.   Go 'way horse.   Shoo.

Stop chomping, stop blowing clouds of heat.
I stare away, increasing
the darkness, inventing an owl, also
white but perhaps oracular

like the bird that flew through the window
the day I spoke in tongues,
   white fire
   white iron
   heat.
But heat brings back the horse, loaded

with things to trade, short, stocky,
not at all tired. So, this is an old landscape,
one I've hidden from myself
because it's stupid.

Dumb.
Doesn't speak, it insinuates a journey
and embarrassed I try to erase
the suddenly obvious owl before it drops a feather,

before a single symbolically meaningful feather
falls. But it's dangerous to imagine
owls, hard to blot them out,
even with chemicals,

scissors may fail, may leave another moon.
The horse lowers its head, eats.
Heat swells from the body and from
the bales of hay laid out

like giant erasers, like desks
in a dark classroom. Still, if I took drugs
this is where I'd go. I can't
banish the stupid white horse

but I can move the moon, divide it,
put it back together.
I can draw any face on it
I like. And the owl leaves the low tree

to sit at my feet (owl on the ground,
never meant to see that!)
More things catch moonlight, come
into being, distant silos,

small acorn crowns, each post moon-washed
and one-sided. It's warm enough here
to do without fire, but
that's it. No story. No arcane

wisdom or poignantly revealed momentous
event. I just like this quiet.
And the owl who opens his one
good eye. The horse

keeps his head in the hay making heat.
I prefer moonlight,
I like the green to be almost black.
I like a lot of space

with nothing going on.
A few white words
and the rim of the milk pail polished
and fine in my dark.

Landscape with Silos

One nail sticking up in a pile of boards,
air bladders from fish brought home for supper,
sugar in green glass bowls,
glittering rattlesnakes.

The palsied ghosts of cloudstained women,
shadows of railroad men far from their homes,
a deep-freeze filled with molasses cookies,
broken concrete, lilacs, thunder.

We drank water from old pipes,
picnicked under windbreaks, peach pits
and eggshells, and in the glove box
roadmaps to the river, to the reservation,

to Fargo and Minot. But no maps
to the silos where men tended missiles so big
we didn't even dream about them.
They didn't scare us, those missiles,

not the men either who rose like bankers,
sat calmly at the counter, starched and pressed.
Keys jingled on their belts.
They ordered root beer and blackbottom pie.

Learning Italian

All of our friends are learning Italian.
They have no plan, no particular plan

to go to Italy, just a vague hope
like when I laid me down to sleep

and aimed at heaven. We're at an age
when people travel, so many

places to go, France is attractive,
and Poland, or if you came back

from China with a baby that would count.
Even riding a bicycle to and fro

in the cool shade, a book tucked
under your arm, French or Polish

or Chinese, is something, but most
of our friends have chosen Italian

which they practice diligently
at lunch tables where only Italian

may be spoken. "The weather is fine."
or "Please call the porter." In the evening

on porches they still practice
"When is the train for Milan?"

Four Truths about Anesthesia

1/

The hole opens, the one in the back of your head,
just above the neck where children love to be tickled.
This porthole opens and sleep tests the air as slow
molecules count themselves into a long plastic tube.
There's smoke moving in the light of the projector
and the gas develops a taste like a lover's tongue.
Calm heat rises, taking you with it. Your soul's
misplaced. Your thoughts are laid out like the
unclaimed dead.

2/

A curtain falls somewhere in the cavity, the
diaphragm relaxes, winds die down and you're
suddenly soft—like the baby in its bath, like raw
sausage or clothes from the dryer. Words you spoke
only an hour ago are as inconsequential now as the
speech of women in Russian novels, Sophia and
Esther in the summerhouse, the young blades gone to
battle. Airy sponges soak up blood and you're quiet—
but at the end you panic, gasp like a drowning man,
fish-mouthed, unlovely and suck in sleep.

3/

The nerves go first, those long wires crossing the
plain of your back are strung with weights at irregular
intervals, sagging, unable to blow in memory's breezes
or transmit the simplest text. You drop the disguise of
your personality, lie slack-faced, unbothered
by intelligence as valves are opened and closed, your
limbs arranged on the clean white tablecloth. Septicemia
sounds in the distance, echoing until the submarine of
your body drops its scope and you sink.

4/

It's a carnival, it's bright hallucinations, a tilt-a-whirl
ride and the small prick barely noticeable among
the helium balloons. The periphery's alight with
fireworks that detonate like giant dandelions and
as your stunned brain scans the midway, neurons
careen down a luminous path where green-masked
barkers offer rigged chances to count backwards, to
sing the national anthem, to say what may have been
left unsaid. And the words ricochet in your skull
—sassafras, sassafras, sassafras.

Road

From here I see it, dark between
Brad Whipple's barn and wobbly
house, the road with that flat flannel
smudge that means the blacktop's
been scooped out by storm or snow
plow, every day more worn away.
Rain's hurt us all but mainly this road,
ours—if the storms keep on it'll wash
clear out, and from down there we must
look small and shabby, house lights
stuttering, frail and dim, but the road
was sound, our triumph, black as boots
(the man we paid to tamp it stopped
some evenings just to look.) So tell me,
why do things get old? Ties and aprons,
now the road which even I can see is
on the brink. You told me how you
watched me walking up past Whipple's
coin-purse cows, his house and barn,
and tried to see the color of my hair
although of course you know the brown
but color doesn't show that far. I was
a stick figure, you said, climbing.

I Work at the Community Center

On Thursdays we have art class. Kids
make paintings for their dads and a lady comes
to explain what a stranger is.

When I asked for a dream of my father
I had night sweats three times in a row.
I tell the children if you love your paintings

they'll love you back but it's a kind of sickness
when you can't dream of your father.
Some nights we have TV. Body counts are

back. The reporter says they've asked for
a ceasefire to bury their dead. I sit in the dark
and think of the names of exotic grasses:

love in a mist and love lies bleeding.

Leonardo Dreams

Loosening the skin like
a robe
I slide from the body clean and alive,
    a silver tuning fork,
sleek,
without opinion
    and move deerlike
into a blue meadow surrounded by winds,
    lucid as the glassblower's
sunlit extrusion.

It's a shift from the flesh
but there's something at work,
something spinning,

and a moment
when my lungs exhale the smell
of lemons,

when the hot coal of the hummingbird's
crown
becomes another eye,
    another way to see things.

Living by the Children's Cemetery

1/

For weeks I've ignored a presence,
stillness
and faceless blue breath on the cellar windows.
But tonight beyond the yard
moon-stained crosses quiver like
delicate antennae.
Before I climb into bed,
I press a hand to the window and feel the cold.

2/

The moon's stuck
in a milk bottle and ancient horse tack
hangs on the porch where my grandfather drank
while upstairs Edith screamed my mother
into this world.
Textbooks say I was there too,
        an incipient presence,
and I want to name that,
what that was. I want to name it
like the stones in the cemetery want to name
something.
Where did we learn to surrender our children
to priests who bless them,
who lift them high
amid incense and smoke and take them
to meet the Holy of Holies?

3/

Ants come out of the earth,
long coded helixes that carry away
what's been lost in the dark.
They try to help me understand the cemetery's work,
      how we must give up
what we cannot mend or keep.
Still, it hurts,
like a fist clenched too long.
We must learn to lie flat,
to enter their darkness
with our hearts and our useless wings
open.

4/

Standing by these small graves in Garrison,
North Dakota
I want some kind of consolation.
I want wisdom.
      And you do too,
you there at the kitchen sink in Sioux Falls,
South Dakota,
in Billings, Montana and Casper,
Wyoming. And you up late in Vermont
and you in the Black Hills of Tennessee.
How do we accept the soil
that fills their mouths?
How do we ever go inside again?

Bedtime Story

The apple, the lips, the drop of blood,
the thorn, the bloom in the young girl's
cheeks. A rosy warmth, you feel the heart,
the rocking motion, blanket's weight.
This is the start of a small dream, lazy
campfire, gypsy song, this is the song
of the peddler's wagon, peek of stocking,
lusty daughter. This is desire lapping the edge,
dark red flowers, smell of smoke. These
are the songs of the drunken men, eating
sausages made from blood. This is you
in your father's arms. Are you dreaming now?
Are you dreaming yet? There's darkness
ahead, shadowy wolves, their jaundiced
eyes, their long slick tongues. Can you hear
the bells, do you feel the pull? The night air
chills, you reach for fire. You see the daughter
sent to the stream, buckets swinging back and
forth. This is a dream. The start of a dream.
Who is the girl? The wolves advance.

Crows

He said John, immediately
the crows appeared.
Not sad, I said, I'm not.

He said, in case of emergency
call. A leaf fell.
We danced until two.
He said he lived over

a truck stop, said,
these particular crows
are trouble's handprint.

I remembered Robert,
before him Michael,
room 208,
wallets on dressers,

in case of emergency
please notify,
the phone rang, black

like crows, sky seeped in,
singed, vagrant.
I don't sing, I said.
I do everything but that.

He said, keep this
in a safe place, said, in case
of emergency.

The fistful of crows flickered,
black, eating holes
in the windows,
a kind of notification,

a kind of emergency,
a kind of slipping away.
And the wallet lay open

on the window,
the glass emptied itself,
a stain in the back
of my throat,

the taste of wet wood.
The windows cracked,
crows flew through

making holes not in the sky,
but in the world.
I said John, I said,
please notify,

there's an emergency.
The crows wheeled
above us, a circular saw.

Learning the Language

There was a pile of words out by the shed,
another spit from the combine's teeth
and words that Ethel said would fuel the nation
in its fight for something large and metal.

Aunt Trini whispered voodoo words as silent
John backed down the drive, and Gram
knew words as bright as rhubarb jam
and brown wet words awash in the Missouri.

Kids heard barge words, baseball words,
the strangled words of wet sheets groaning
through the ringer. There were stately Sunday
words swinging from steeples like flags

in a thunderstorm, but they were lost mostly
among the snickers of the high-school boys,
their pussywords, those ritual recitations
meant to conjure what was missing.

The Poem Ventures Out

*The light on dark scumble consists
of scrubby strokes
that move in different directions.*

[*Complete Guide to Acrylic Painting* —Weldon Blake]

The Poem Listens to Its President on TV

O, it wants to be beautiful,
to be naked and necessary, it
gestures toward sparrows,
hums under its breath, but
the poem's picking up brutish
habits, bared teeth in the bathroom
mirror, a vaguely Caliginous grin.
The poem shuts its eyes, thinks
Hannibal was a boy mad for power
who loved elephants and feared
slave girls, a boy who licked
the tips of his arrows before he
put them to flight. So the poem
presses the mute, but it can still
see the face, it thinks of Alexander's
famous dream, his mother's head
on another man's pike.
And Aristotle was Alexander's teacher,
it thinks. That's the kind of thing
that makes the poem uneasy, the way
Alexander brought a "love of learning"
to the world with his bloody sword,
wacking at people, bashing them,
their soft bits of flesh exposed to the air,
crusting, turning black.
He saved those people from their chieftains
and their ignorance, tore
sons from their mothers and laid harsh leather
harnesses on their bloodied
shoulders so they could pull the carts.

After the State of the Union
the Poem Goes Out for Coffee

At the Rebel Café the inmates materialized.
Everyone said the President looked medicated.

And of themselves: "I'm a little off today.
I'm a little off."

Sam's run into some luck, an inheritance,
                    twenty or thirty thousand.
"I'm starting a small press." he says, "All I have to do
is keep my head together."

Jeffrey's gotten a tip.
A good tip.
        He just needs his medical papers.

In the back booth the bald guy asks,
"Do you speak Mandarin or mandolin?"

This is a question that also concerns the poem.

                    Across the street the stained glass
                        windows continue their
                            slow melt.

The Poem as Tease

All she has to do is crook her little finger
and you follow. Light trickles away,
the stairs narrow and darken but you follow
while sensible grown-ups get to brush
their teeth or head to the kitchen to get those
dishes done.

Is this smart? And do you think it's part
of some grand scheme, that this time
you'll uncover what's under those unlettered
images cluttering memory?

Why can't you forget the wallpaper
by the bed where you dreamt of the golden girl
feeding her father's ducks. No one cares
about that. Forget the skate key, and the way
the evening sky invented surgeries,
carving its space in you.

You'll never enter a darkness as whole
and strange as your mother's breath after the party
or feel heat like her palm searing you as
she brushed the bangs from your face.
But you love it there, half-light, half-opened door.
And the poem knows that.

The Poem Takes the GRE

> "*Do not choose an answer simply because*
> *it is true.*" GRE Instructions

1/

The poem wakes her when
it begins to snow.
               What snows?
          What it?

The best answer is the one
that most accurately and completely
answers the question being asked.

E.g., the poem wakes her when
          the sky/world/cloud
begins to snow.
It's snowing and it's getting light.   Both.

2/

From the window she sees the world
lit from the core.
          False. She sees a mangy snow-covered
          yard.
But how does she see it?
          She sees it lit, which raises the question—is
memory necessary for love?

3/

She's staring through glass at a distant
snowman. She sees

     a) his upraised arms,
     b) his hard-headedness,
     c) his accurate voicelessness.

Be certain you understand exactly
what is being asked.
              Check for irony, humor and the like.

The Poem's Put Under Surveillance

6:00 a.m.

Subject is up before the furnace kicks in,
lingers in the vicinity of the dreamer, glances at the
pen and paper, wills a half-waked hand to move.

6:23 a.m.

Subject takes small breaths. Waits. Appears to
ponder. File indicates the poem weaves imperfectly
as the Navajo. Subject does not appear to be able to
wake the dreamer.

7:30 a.m.

Subject sighted entering dreamer. Becomes
not so much dream as meta-dream, voice-over, the
perfume of the dream. The dreamer sucks at it,
appears to want the air of it deep in her lungs.

7:45 a.m.

At the moment of waking, subject sinks, is
locked in the body, lost to view. Sound recordings
indicate bloodrush, bonegrind. Subject appears to be
outweighed. Oppressed. Modus operandi: informants
advise the poem waits on opportunity.

8:50 a.m.

Reviewing analyst advice: the poem has much in common with the virus. Quiescence. A need for catalyst. Eruption. Agents are advised to watch for agitation, a shortened attention span. Sharp teeth. Typically there are lesions and a spreading rash.

12:30 p.m.

Appears subject may have misjudged its body. Body looks at calendar. Note: tennis date. Also note: increased activity in facial nerves. Twitching.

1:00 p.m.

Body sits down, gets out notebook, favorite pen. Audio indicates body mumbling—*what am I doing? I don't have a thought in my head.* Attention all units. This is it. It's going down. It's making its move…

The Poem Sits in with the Band

1/

Time   is a problem   parameter.
    Carve it   in a personal way.

Consider the weight of sound
        the way crickets chirp   in pulse fields.

Did you just think: but the blues begins in the third
strain?

2/

Whatever the meter is,
               divide it.

     A particular zone
with a set of pitches signals a need
     for gestural work.

Learn to sabotage pulse.
        The polyrhythmic aspects
will become more
defined   because time is
    a problem parameter.

Neurons can't quit.   Firing.

3/

Never use these words:
Tick. Beat. Rhythm.   Swing.
Never use these words:
          throb   accent   tempo.

(I like   all my food   on one plate.)

The Poem Goes to the Kitchen to Empty
the Dishwasher But Ends Up Praying

Grace must be like this sunstreak
on the linoleum,
          this unexpected elegance,
a rope of gold up which we pull ourselves
          amazed, having thought it gone
that thing which penetrates,
          which chooses us,
which illumines one moment
          so that the book of hours opens
to a single letter, loved
          and labored over,
lavished and extravagantly gilded—say
          a mystic vowel embellished in blue,
a hint of scarlet and in the center
          nothing,
the white suddenly framed
          as a field of Queen Anne's lace
or the snow-draped Steppes,
          door to another geography.

Let me move through it,
this door, let me see the monk bent
over the table, his brushes of camel's hair
and mink, his window stabbed
by sun, a lance that leaves a wound
of gold.

Transfiguration: marked change, a sudden
          emanation.

A page. Linoleum.
                    Amen.

Poem in the Dark

You wake hungry.
It's hot.
Outside mockingbirds lecture the moon.
You know you won't sleep
but here's your consolation,

      at this hour no one's lost.

Not your father slumped in his autumn
gold recliner
or your sister aglow in the oxygen
tent. There's Mr. Hanstrom
still mowing his lawn

and back on the farm eternal cats
circle the separator. Uncle Earl still
straddles his John Deere and Ethel sits
at the Singer.

Somewhere Jim's playing his clarinet.

In the dark you hear him perfectly.

The Poem Enters the Talent Show

Your baton is thin and shiny. There's
a circle on the stage. You must stay inside
the circle until your routine is finished.

You step into the circle willingly
as they put your music on the machine.
The music's round. It's a circle.

The needle's a diamond extracting the music.
Most diamonds come from Africa. Some have been
deep inside the rectums of the diggers.

He was found out, the one who cut
this diamond from rock, but diamond-tipped
needles free music from vinyl

and Ella Fitzgerald is some of the music
they free. You get tired. When you get to the end
you think there will be an answer to all

your questions. But there's just the circle
and what's outside the circle. You hurl your
baton high, hoping you can catch it.

The Poem Thinks about Beauty

Sundown.
Along the county road
old sheds exhale and take on shine.

Trees lace wine-stained fingers—
even thistles grow more purple.

So this is beauty.
Is this is where I take my stand?

Will the rhythm of that branch
/ scraping / scraping /
tell me how to read the headlines? How to bury
the child found in the dumpster?

I need to hold to something,
the way these trees hold their dark shapes as bats
stir and witty toad calls are squelched
by the boot of the hunter.

Yes, I know everything's obliterated
by the hack and saw
of the world preparing to enter another darkness
but I'm tired of waiting. I want the angels
to come down.

I want the angels to inhabit us,
to enter our bodies whole,
suffused by our darkness, stained
and staining us till the ache in our backs
is decent.   And wholly between the blades.
Sharp.
Like a sprouting.

The Plot Thickens

So we played until dark,

the poem doing its little blind tapping act.

I made critical inquiries into obsolete rites,
disputable etymologies,

the poem claimed the museum of ultimate mysteries
made us strangers to our own

clothes. I said, but isn't ice skating really
a dream function?

Relax, the poem told me,
          remember these are words—

something you can alter,
                              later.

Visitations

My father took me as far as he could that summer.

[Thomas McGrath]

Home Movies

The shape of the head which
you see from the backseat of the Buick,
a corona of smoke and a roll of fat
above the stiff white collar.

Then the lap where you sink into "Black Beauty",
more smoke, a watch ticking.

Later, sled runners on snow,
a man pulling you, the long coat and hat
        make him look like
all the other fathers.

His eyes stare right into yours,
        but you can't really remember that.

                    ~

Later, normal life,
everything according to a carpenter's square.

You think of him standing under
a street light,

and the Fourth of July when
he put you on his shoulders and galloped
across the dark lawns.

                    ~

This is Red Lodge.
Your horse is Duchess, a golden horse,
a big gold horse. The man
on the brown horse is Daddy.
            His back's wet.

This is a good place.
He brought you here, drove you up
the Going-to-the-Sun Road.

You must be fourteen when
you find him slumped in the autumn gold
recliner,
            the bourbon gone,
medical books splayed across his lap.

He reads to learn what it means,
this prognosis.
            Is he bathed in the lamplight?

And when he dies,
when he sets the car ablaze to end it,
            amnesia.

The need to wander out into the blizzard,
            into snow,
                        with its anti-convulsant effects,
without obligatory electrical activity.

Without memory,
            or lack of memory.

~

Then somehow you're grown.
      Your mother's come to see your kids.
Before she leaves, she says
      I thought you might want this,

hands you the can heavy with film,
"Whitefish Lake, 1959."
      That was the summer you learned
to ski, Dad in the boat facing back to film it.

He's got you dipping into rough water,
but later he shifts his aim to the shoreline,

      tree, after tree, after tree, after tree

and he can't get enough of it.

The Barn Holds the Sky Up

Most night we can't sleep. We sit out
till the moon shows. If it's late,
if I know the kids won't wake, I strip
and lay full out on the grass.
Orion's up there, a big professor
in his lecture hall. "Tonight," he says,
"I have a great deal of material
to cover." And the Bible says a good man
loves the light, only the wicked love
what's hidden but I think that's just talk.
Just talk I think, and when the grass
is wet like this, and cool, I feel empty.
Free almost. Some say the moon makes things
look strange. I think it lets us see how
strange things are, scarecrows in
their wedding clothes, the way light snows
on trees. The Bible says the sun's got
one kind of glory, the moon another.
I see best in moon-lit glory.

"Go down, a clutch of feathers…"

A Canticle to the Waterbirds,
Brother Antoninus

I asked myself then what it was
I'd been, that sober different thing
no longer someone's anything
and not a steak, not good as that.

I asked where was it—where that
place where what I'd heard was
soundlessness itself, a thing which
knew itself more than I could know

anything. And why the bland
linoleum here under what you'd
kissed as mouth. Why light's grand
show lost, black here, black. And

not a hush—too loud a word
for what I'd thought I'd never hear.

Sepia Print

We called the child "she loved the doll."
The name of the mother is likewise gone,
but they're our fabled ancestors,
we know they crossed the oceans.
The trail to the names is overgrown,
one day the hasp on the trunk just broke
and no one kept the great aunt's earrings,
no one kept the small girl's doll.
Some say we came from Austria.
Others claim it was Hungary,
by now the churchyard stones are smooth.
By now the records are kept by mice.
Some think we came from Hungary.
Others claim it was Austria,
of course the small girl's doll was lost
and no one kept the great aunt's jewels.
The hasp on the trunk was old, it broke,
the trail to the names grew faint and wild.
Oh, we love that they crossed the water,
our heroes, our daring ancestors,
but no one can tell me the mother's name
or claim the girl who rocks that doll.

"It's about Heaven"

These are the words she said
and this is what I know about the shape of words:
    if you drop the lower jaw a soft sound comes out.

But we have been all day at the specialist
and this is what he knows, how he looks and what he
cares about:

    a) studies have been done
    b) he wears a bow tie with a sense of purpose
    c) he tells her there's a way to handle the
        depression/impression/compression.

Then he conducts the interview:

    She says   *I have been leavened all my life.*
    He hears "I've been eleven all my life."

    She says   *The angels flew, clouds purpled and
                darkened.*
    He hears "Then angles skewed, I was
                disheartened."

I know the pain she carries is in a little bucket.
It's like a bucket of pennies—she can't buy much with
it but she won't put it down.

Still, the specialist is happy.
He says the new medication has a 50% chance of
working,
that we are halfway to heaven again, so

we ride home on the bus.
I relax my jaw, say "halo" and "sparrow."
Outside, God has placed strategic clouds.
Her neck aches from looking up.

Visitation

Small knots of form, grey against
grey,

an unnerving calm at the window,
long crows
        not going anywhere.

Everything concentrated, like
metal in the blood.

The dead lose their ages,
                their eyelashes,
                their bright ideas.

Shiny fingers curl
as if they want me to hear something.

Maybe a joke.

Family Resemblance in Two Parts

1/

When I pressed my thumb
into the black-inked

sponge and rolled it carefully
on the sheriff's clean

white paper, I realized
I'd made a miniature portrait

of my grandmother,
Edith Boots.

The bare bulb, the jeweled
fruit jars, the haloed

smell of fried potatoes,
it was all there.

And later when the deputy
took my picture, when he said

don't smile, face front,
now turn, it was like

standing on a coffee table
in a curtained North Dakota

living room, Grandma
on her knees, lips tight,

mouth full of pins,
hemming my summer dresses.

2/

Since his mug was always
shadowed by a cap

or buried in the side
of a cow, it was

a miracle she recognized
the face of Allen

Conklin, my uncle,
in the sweet potato she dug

from the garden
in West Calvin County.

We set it in the window,
with a sense of ceremony,

of mystery, with
no blessing but the dirt

clinging to the root
hairs. He cracked our toes

for fun and hardly ever
went to church,

but it looked
just like him, I swear.

At the End of the Century
the Evening Strollers
Make Their Final Adjustments

Sinister dwarves abuse their servants even here, but
much goes unremarked when a traveling puppet show's
in town. At dusk the Place du St. Mark congratulates
itself on its fine representations of majesty. Tiny
generals on tiny rearing horses dominate the fountain
as the evening strollers arrange their scarves and
head for cafes amid dancing dogs, old women bent
on mass and the pigeons at their eternal buffet.

What a beautiful entanglement! Legs, umbrellas,
and the waiters' long white aprons. It's not quite dark,
just purpling dusk, sky awash in the invisible descent
of the sun. Bats and gargoyles circle the cathedral,
the card players lay down their hands. Ce soir
Monsieur La Plage occupies the corner table.

Long Distance

When she called I said, there have been
a number of medical breakthroughs, have you
checked with your pharmacologist? She said
she'd been reading the cards, said the stars
were ominous. I told her it helped to do
visualization therapy: imagine yourself riding
an elephant across the Savannah. I keep thinking,
she said, that I'm sprouting wings. I keep thinking
the annular eclipse is some kind of halo.
It helps, I said, to breathe in slowly and think of
a safe place. Lately, she said, I've had art on my
mind. Have you heard of Hieronymous Bosch?
I've been thinking, she told me, about Plato's Cave
and also Van Gogh's Potato Diggers. She told me
she was considering a move, maybe Cleveland or San
Francisco. I said have you checked to see
what's covered on your insurance plan? Some
of them allow acupuncture and reflexology.
She told me the visual disturbances had decreased.
All she had now was a little fortress spectra.
She said she didn't want to be swallowing pills
all day. But, I said, you can't be adjusting your
meds. You need to be under a doctor's supervision.
I've been spending time at the beach,
she told me. Under the pier. It's quiet there, well
not quiet but the noise is white noise. I told her
I'd heard white noise could be effective,
that they had machines for that, some of which
were covered by insurance. I'd read a study
where in conjunction with appropriate medication
white noise was quite effective. Last week,
she told me, I went to church, I went to the Baptist
church she said, where people have conviction.

That's good, I said, it helps to be under a doctrine's
supervision. *Good Morning America* had a show
on that, how religion makes people happier.
Fuck happy, she said, I just need a way to cope.
Gospel music can be a lot like white noise,
she told me, it's a lot like standing under the pier.

L.A.'s Millennial Love Song

Seismologists say things are stable
but we know different.
            Feel the new laws?
They dog the heart like hunger
at the offramp, like drunks
at Union Station,
            like rain that chants
no money. No money.
No money.

The drought's over, tuberculin clouds
explode. Each bus stop sprouts its teenage
mom, her Tiny Tears coughing up our
            bad dreams.

Caltrans warns of dangerous parents holding
the hands of their children as they head north
to clean our houses.

Our streets are lined with Tarot cards,
crystal balls, massage parlors.
Psychic hotlines tie up the State.
We peek out from behind shuttered windows.

Some say hardness of heart can
shake the earth. Some say it's coming.
It's coming. It's coming.

If your house has a candle, light it.
If the baby cries, pick her up.

Leo as Sketch Artist

A man sells birds so the rich can
breakfast, birds

so the poor can feast. Leonardo buys
but does not breakfast.

He carries the cages to meadows where,
pencil in hand

he frees them to watch as they rise.
And it's not like

the dreams in which he flies, not like
those phantoms

the tick-tock brain concocts. It's fast
and full of effort,

bodies wed to earth but persuaded
by wings. Again he watches,

his eye the camera, freezing each frame,
adjusting for light

and catching something, downstroke
to tail wind, sinew

strength and muscle mass. Each time
he catches something,

the pencil scratching, his eyes tearing
like a madman,

like a man who won't eat what is
good for him.

Granddaughter

You come in your boat,
the body, the gate.
We meet at the dock, you
come in your boat, come
daily—like shrimp.
We meet at the dock,
the water awash, your body
a boat, my ankles are light,
but the circle grows large as
the darkness comes,
as it comes to my boat.

Your body's a boat
     My body's a boat.
We meet at the dock.

The Shrines of Paradise

At night the children lay their heads
in the laps of their thirsty mothers
who tell them the story, how God
made it, the Garden, with everything
His people would ever need.

~

The New York Times reports that
scholars are closing in on the exact
location of the Garden of Eden.
They're pretty sure they've found it.

~

We've been at war here for two years.
Of course the damage to the original
Garden was not done by us. There have
always been wars here. War after war.

~

Each night thirsty mothers cradle their
treasures, their children. They rock
them and tell them a story, how God
made the Garden with everything.
Everything.

Visiting Dave

We call it a kind of capability:
You just slide from the self—then fly.
—Carol Muske-Dukes

We've come to the valley of skulls
and moonlight. They smile in toothless
wonder. There's expectation in the air,
but they're not anxious. They're like a crowd
at an execution, dull-eyed, with a ticket

for the show. We shake in the tumbrel,
taste salt in the air. It's not that we're
unprepared. Molecule by molecule our bodies
moved toward this moment. The mind
knows now, there is no mind-body

problem. The body knows it has no shoes.
Impulse can't move your spine,
muscles relax and you say you want to go,
but the hospital's got plans and doors
that lock. They say "we can fix him"

and teach you to eat, to watch TV.
David, we can't save you from these
mercies, can't send you off with music
and the family gathered. Listen Dave,
we love you. We say, fly David. Fly.

Grief for Three Fathers

1.

The sleeping bed is white like
a symbol but it's not,
it's just a white bed in a blue room
and across the way the louvers
slant the light coming through.
Oh poor little father on your knees
to wake me
to say good bye.
And who knew this?
Not the reporter from the gazette.

2.

Second small father, your hand
was meat and safety.
Outside the war raged.
I lay still, as if I was already dead
but you came to rescue me.
You raised me up.
            I said *Don't you know—*
                we're not on the same side?

3.

In the west, a great sun sets.
God and Abraham Lincoln suffer by
comparison.
In the west, this great slow setting.
Your revolver's cocked.

Within the Porcelain Theater

Reality leaves a lot to the imagination.

[John Lennon]

The First Message

Rooms of darkness nest, one within
the other—in us they nest
and even stars can't light them.

They're part of us,
                    like bone
and most of what we own, we earn
moving in that dark.
          I feel for the next stair
(darling, sleep)
stringing lanterns where I walk
but it's not about metaphor.

This poem's about the cold
                    pushing me back into bed,
                              into - darling sleep.

The OED: "Sex is Indeclinable"

She balanced the cake on the edge of the plate,
and the plate in the palm of her hand
and in the cup the tea, burning—

so you said yes. You trusted the body
which seems to know so much,
which hungers and eats.
Tires and sleeps.

Beyond the window the day bent to the earth's
fat curve, to the yellow-straw sky,
cello-deep afternoon.

And didn't you love the strange light,
waking suddenly in the cradle
of your own flesh?

Separate Houses

They grew to be good neighbors, friends
who gossiped by the backyard fence, they
helped each other's kids through tough years,
cheered at track meets, called them "dear"
and when one traveled kept in touch,
brought in the mail, watered lawns though
he thought hers too manicured and let his grow
to shaggy silver (lovely silver). Falls they
watched as colors changed and not surprised
at evening's tiresome timeliness went in and
closed their separate doors, at separate windows
looking up but only at the stars, they knew
that much and night came as it does. It must.

Sleep Therapy

Under the bed what's
Battened down?
Sleep loosens the lock.

In the dream a bird with a broken
Beak. In the dream, I become
Air-o-plane.

To dream of flying is classic
Among children.
They describe the missing

Roof tiles. So my life is twice
As long as the one
I share with you.

Tell me.
What is it to know?
The voice says *practice, practice.*

The Artist at the Kitchen Table

paints the salt shaker against the green
curtain. She paints it as if it's
her mother walking into the forest.

Then she paints the silver
pill box and the telephone that grins
like God not ringing.

There was so much to be numb
about.   Still, the mail arrived.
Children returned
        (and did not return)

from school. The doctor offered
soundless white in the silver
box which the artist paints and repaints

as if she can resuscitate snow.

Four Answers to Questions About Insanity

The Nurse Answers

We distill it, break it down to this last simplicity.
Scissors snip the tags as strong arms put the show
on wheels. The outside world has complications,
clocks to wind, trains, buses, school girls clutch-
ing algebra to their new breasts. Even geraniums
need tending and there are too many people in
the streets, disturbing newspapers climbing up
the pumping legs. But here, in the quiet dark,
we float down alabaster hallways, providers of
magazines. You will learn to love the sails of
our hats.

The Poet Answers

Winter's big in Ohio. Few trees, frozen wetlands.
For color we have three browns, two blues. That's
why we live here, where standing still's a kind of
action. A meditation that shoots you through to
the other side. Poems! Not wives whose tropical
thighs like babyfat snow obscure the hillside's
fine severity. Poems! Not children, their wet nose-
clouds pressed against our office windows. In
here we write of marshes, lurid dreams, water
flowing out of control. Many of us have translated
Chinese poems full of orchids, drunkenness and
sexual longing.

The Mermaid Answers

They love us, something about us, as we float here
beneath the surface. Opal crescents mark our fore-
heads, grey-green oyster beds from which we rise.
We are their tarot cards. We sing the I Ching, our
curling leaves house mystery. Here we wait, we
wait to feel, we wait to know, and to begin. We
wait forever, our song is waiting, our prayer is
waiting, our gift is waiting. In our waiting is their
freedom, for we do nothing. Nothing at all. We do
not know all that we hold, we do not know all
that they love. They love our hair moving in the
water. They love our hips moving in their hands.

The Inmate Answers

Cleveland. Boxed up and manageable. I like it.
Will we have ice cream for lunch? There are doors
that go out, but I don't use them, I like their
windows, strung with wire that cuts the world up
even smaller, some blocks are blue, some are green.
(The white ones are the clouds.) In the Rec Room we
have puzzles and students come from Oberlin
to sing us "Michael Row Your Boat Ashore."
I think the long-haired girl wants to marry me.
She likes the view. In here it isn't Spring or Winter.
Everything is windows. I like the small trees
squatting in them. I like the birds singing in the glass.

The Second Message

It's as strange as the sleep of plants
or saddened silk, thick on thrice-plowed fields,
covering famous bones like
snow whose

flakes, whose curve tends toward the infinite,
the tabular, but it's close, close as incest.
Demeter's still plucking
her geese.

Within the Porcelain Theater

Set

White walls, white ceiling, white floor,
      rectangular and like
this luminous sheet of paper restfully
      blank. White the way
a color wheel is white and on the table
      a water glass. There's
a feather on the floor, another on the
      window sill, a ladybug
crawls across the table. You can see
      that nothing's obscured
or guessed at here. Water so clear
      it represents itself.

Lighting

Less than full illumination,
      (as if threatened by storm
or milk sickness).

Our Protagonist

He's been at the table for weeks
      and the moon is up.
His bag's packed, two clean white
      shirts, a tooth brush
and the address book with the number
      of every woman he ever
wanted to touch. Just touch,
      he thinks. The pale clock's
still, but a stirring threatens.

This wanting's been going on
a long time and see his toe tapping?
A small movement, but
character begins in movement, in
gesture, a toe tap or
the slide of a hand across the table.
There's a shift in
the body's weight when we rise.

The Chorus

We're trying to get a glimpse of ourselves,
the mirror aslant in the chamber.
We walk slow halls of sleep, the slippers,
the white gowns making it all a bit

difficult. We're anxious, afraid the world's
a walnut after all, that we're the dolls
our children wanted for Christmas
and we want science, some clarification.

Like plants, our breath is quiet. Our eyes
open but we can't wake up. Who hasn't
been alone a long time? We weep
internally like plumbing under the sink.

Most nights we sleep from four till
five, till the flatline dawn releases us.
When we pull back the curtain we get
a good look at the cloudless summer sky.

Still, we're afraid there's a walnut shell
around the heart's blue membrane,
we're afraid our hands will get hurt,
we're afraid the body will desert us.

The Ingénue

What's your belief about the nature
of the body? She gathers her ritual objects

and tries to cultivate a reverence
for explanation. Sometimes her thoughts

are unbroken horses. She's glad
she never had to live on the streets.

Nights return her to the meadow where
they buried her complicated five-year-old self.

She loves blues and satire, a didactic
combination, but edgy, like sacrificial

wine. She believes objects receive their
beauty via gesture, via how they are held.

She believes in love hunger, the power
of black dirt and dragonflies, the children

chasing after them. Even though she
found broken teeth on the ground.

How much truth did you expect from the living?
She believes the cage is never locked.

Act One

Of course they find the garden.
            See them there,
how they're comparing notes?
            She says she dreams
of swans and teeth. She says cocaine

and flour. She covets snake
root, as poisonous plants have
         heart-shaped leaves, claims
to know charms for protection:
         white of the egg
and white of the eye.
         He tells her he once saw
seven seraphs descend on
         electromagnetic waves,
says now he knows it was only an
         excitation of the retina
caused by a flock of white owls.
         Just then, lightning.
Lightning and precious stones,
         marcasite, white pyrite.
And who can fight nature?
         Already they're dancing.
Already her sexual hair falls on his
         angled shoulder.

Musical Interlude

There are witching songs for milking
         and working songs
for the stretching of cloth. She loves
         the tremolo of birds,
dawn's lazy gesture of communion.
         He loves a white cloth
spread on the table. At night there are
         drums and ivory
moths who fan their distant mother.

Intermission

gills snow egrets ice
soap milk frost geese

chalk bread wedding sugar
ivory igloo skin pearl

goat sky hanky seashell
lightning crystal egg owl

flour christmas blank rabbit
pillow corpse silk wine

laundry hope magic heat
tooth habit clover bloodless

Act Two

Dinner parties. Vacations
in the Poconos.

But he begins to think she has a head
like a question mark.

She starts to wonder what you can do
in a small space.

They read books on heartache, its ease
and abatement

as under the sink the plumbing weeps.
Who hasn't been alone

a long time or threatened by milk
sickness?

The Extras and the Cameo

In town an annoyance of angels, the streets
filling with bread crumbs that

settle like dandruff on the corporate
shoulders of America.

And in the parks a slack-jawed populace
gathers, falls to the ground

not in adoration, just sleepy, sun
reaching the marrow.

Balloons of hope rise as old men float by
on vernacular breezes.

O pearls of saliva, O featherings of sound.
O angels who won't work,

tell time, wear shoes. Unwelcome squatters
swell the lines

at the coffee bars. And God turns his pockets
inside out.

Act Three

He's gone to Cleveland to sell real estate.
And if he feels that way, she thinks,

why not? She shimmies, shrugs off
the burden of fertility. Walking at dawn

she meets a yearling buck, tries not
to make too much of it. Then he calls

to say he's taken his exams, says
certification is heavenly.

If there was a heaven, she thinks,
there'd be dragonflies there.

Finale

Single file, our white gowns open
in back, how perfectly formed we were
in the mythical garden.

Now we're in this parade, our white
gowns flapping and this one carries
a treatise, that one two black pots.

A third whistles through his teeth
and we're all marching in our gowns,
our uniforms, our choir robes.

The landscape accepts us like ants at
a picnic, savants who must move to think
and we keep moving in our gowns

the color of new teeth as overhead
snow geese waver sharing their lofty
direction. Still, we feel necessary.

Our children require lunch money.
There are highways to maintain and
the curtained election booths.

We feel we are about something, although
we're in this strange procession,
getting sleepy, perhaps imagining
our robes flaring out like wings.

Dreams after Jean's Reading

Halfway through her life, my
grandmother could vote, late
baby on her spotted arm she entered
the curtained election booth.

⁓

The girl could not see, she needed
to fix that, she lay still as stone
on the table and
opened her eyes to the light.

⁓

Late at night, light
beneath the bathroom door,
my husband's pencil scratching.
Small boy learning to skate.

⁓

What I will not see, sees me.
What I will not see, sees me.
Sees me.
Sees me.
Razors of light.